WHOLE WHEAT
FOR FOOD STORAGE

THE TRAVELING GOURMAND SERIES

1. *The Gluten-Free Way: My Way*, by William Maltese & Adrienne Z. Milligan
2. *Back of the Boat Gourmet Cooking: Afloat—Pool-Side—Backyard*, by Bonnie Clark & William Maltese
3. *William Maltese's Wine Taster's Diary: Spokane/Pullman Washington Wine Region*, by William Maltese
4. *In Search of the Perfect Pinot G! Australia's Mornington Peninsula: William Maltese's Wine Taster's Guide #2*, by A. B. Gayle & William Maltese
5. *Whole Wheat for Food Storage: Recipes for Unground Wheat*, by Michael R. Collings & Judith Collings

WHOLE WHEAT FOR FOOD STORAGE

RECIPES FOR UNGROUND WHEAT

The Traveling Gourmand, Book Five

MICHAEL R. COLLINGS

& JUDITH COLLINGS

THE BORGO PRESS
MMXI

WHOLE WHEAT FOR FOOD STORAGE

Copyright © 1980, 2011 by Michael R. Collings & Judith Collings
Originally published under the title, *Whole Wheat Harvest*

FIRST BORGO PRESS EDITION

Published by Wildside Press LLC

www.wildsidebooks.com

DEDICATION

For

***Michaelbrent
Erika
Ethan
and
Kendra***

Who endured...

CONTENTS

INTRODUCTION 9
MAIN COURSES 11
SOUP-'N'-SANDWICHES. 75
DESSERTS 85
BREAKFASTS 89
SAUCES, GRAVIES, GARNISHES 93
AFTERWORD: On Living with Wheat 103
NOTES AND PERSONAL RECIPES 109
INDEX TO RECIPES BY NAME 115
INDEX TO RECIPES BY COURSES 119
INDEX TO RECIPES BY PRIMARY FOOD
    GROUPS 123
ABOUT THE AUTHORS 127

INTRODUCTION

THIS BOOK IS DESIGNED primarily to answer a perennial question asked by anyone interested in whole-grain wheat as a potential food: "What can I do with it?" The recipes in this book, with few exceptions, call for cooked whole-grain wheat, rather than cracked wheat or whole-wheat flour, simply because many people interested in supplementing their daily diets with wheat are not able to purchase mills or grinders. As a result, there are no bread, biscuit, cake, or cookie recipes included; other excellent books can provide these. Instead, we have tried to collect a variety of offerings, ranging from quick breakfasts, to soup and sandwiches, to one-dish casserole, to impressive entrees, all having in common their incorporation of whole-grain wheat into daily cooking plans.

Whole-grain wheat is itself remarkably simple to prepare. The easiest method is as follows:

COOKED WHEAT

Boil 1 cup whole wheat in ⅔ cups water for 15 minutes; allow to soak overnight. This provides roughly 2 cups cooked whole wheat for using in cooking.

Any remaining wheat may be stored in a closed container in the refrigerator for several days.

We have tried each of the recipes in this book and have found them tasty, exciting, and often unusual adjuncts to our diet. We have been instructed, "Wheat for Man"; this book is one attempt at following that injunction.

MAIN COURSES

GARDEN CASSEROLE

2 cups cooked wheat
1 cup cooked vegetables
2 T onion
3 T butter or margarine
3 T flour
1 t salt
¼ t pepper
2 cups whole milk
1 cup cut-up meat (or canned meat)
2 slices bacon, cooked
½ cup shredded cheese
½ cup bread crumbs
1 t butter or margarine

Pour vegetables into a casserole dish. Top with cooked wheat. Sauté onions in butter in a small skillet. Blend in flour and seasonings. Cook until bubbly, remove from heat and stir in milk. Return to heat and boil 1 minute, stirring constantly. Add cut up meat. Pour the mixture over the vegetables and wheat. Top with cheese and bread crumbs mixed with melted butter. Garnish with crumbled bacon.

Bake at 350 degrees for 25 minutes.

Serves 4.

KRAUT CASSEROLE

1 can drained sauerkraut (16 oz.)
1 can applesauce (16 oz.)
1 cup cooked wheat
1 clove garlic, minced
¼ t pepper
4 frankfurters
5 heat-and-serve sausages

Combine the first five ingredients in a frying pan or electric skillet. Simmer covered, stirring occasionally, for 30 minutes. Score franks ¼ inch deep and arrange them across the top of the sauerkraut mixture. Sprinkle finely chopped sausage (pre-cooked) over the franks. Simmer an additional 15 minutes.

Serves 4-6.

SAUSAGE CASSEROLE

1 cup cooked wheat
1 cup cooked lima beans
1 can tomatoes (16 oz.)
1 can carrots (drained)
¼ cup sautéed onions
8 breakfast sausages, pre-cooked and sliced

Layer ingredients in a casserole dish, beginning with wheat and ending with the sausage slices.

Bake at 350 degrees for 25-30 minutes.

Serves 4-6.

RAINY-DAY PICNIC CASSEROLE

2 cups cooked wheat
1 can pork and beans
3 frankfurters, sliced long-wise
1 can whole kernel corn, drained
3 breakfast sausages, cooked and sliced
2 cups corn chips
2 cups shredded cheese

Layer wheat on the bottom of a casserole dish.

Mix the pork and beans, frankfurter slices, and corn. Spoon over wheat. Top with sausage slices, corn chips, and cheese.

Bake at 450 degrees until thoroughly warm and the cheese melts.

Serves 4-6.

FIVE-LAYER BAKE

1 can beans, drained
1 can corned beef hash or roast beef hash
1 cup cooked wheat
1 can cream of mushroom soup, undiluted
¼ cup mayonnaise
1 t prepared mustard
¼ cup bread crumbs
½ cup shredded cheese

Layer beans, hash, and wheat. Combine mushroom soup, mayonnaise, and prepared mustard and spoon over wheat layer. Top with mixture of bread crumbs and cheese.

Bake at 350 degrees for 30 minutes.

Serves 4-6.

SAUSAGE-'N'-ONIONS

1 can whole kernel corn (reserve liquid)
1 cup onion slices
1 cup cooked wheat
8 oz. breakfast sausages (diced)
3 T butter
2 T parsley flakes
3 hard-boiled eggs (sliced) water
3 T milk powder
2 T flour

Layer corn and onions in a casserole dish. Fry sausage bits, adding wheat, and simmer 5 minutes. Layer over onion. Heat 2 cups liquid (from corn, adding water as necessary). Add butter. Blend milk powder and flour and add gradually to heated water. Bring to a boil, then add eggs and parsley. Pour over mixture in casserole.

Bake at 350 degrees for 25 minutes.

Serves 4-6.

BUTTON CASSSEROLE

2 cups cooked wheat
2 frankfurters, cut into ¼ inch slices
2 cups stewed tomatoes
1 can pork and beans
1 small can tomato sauce
1 t chili powder
1 t onion flakes
¼ t sage powder
½ cup cheese cubes

Pour wheat into a 2-qt. casserole dish. Layer in frankfurter buttons. Mix remaining ingredients in a medium saucepan. Heat slowly until cheese melts. Pour over wheat and franks. Top with additional frankfurter slices.

Bake at 400 degrees for 20-25 minutes.

Serves 4-6.

LASAGNA

3 cups cooked wheat
1 t garlic flakes
2 sausages, finely chopped
1 can tomato paste
1 can tomatoes (20 oz.)
½ t salt
½ t pepper
½ t oregano
1 package lasagna noodles
1½ cups diced Swiss cheese
12 oz. cottage cheese

Combine wheat, garlic flakes, sausage in a skillet and brown. Add seasonings, tomato paste and tomatoes, and allow to simmer 10 minutes. Cook noodles according to package directions. Drain. Spoon ⅓ of the mixture into a baking pan, then layer ½ noodles, cottage cheese, ⅓ wheat mixture, remaining noodles, ½ Swiss cheese, remaining wheat mixture and remaining cheese.

Bake at 350 degrees for 30-40 minutes.

Serves 4-6.

DORITOS BAKE

3 cups cooked wheat
1 can tomatoes (20 oz.)
¼ cup brown sugar
2 T vinegar
2 T soy sauce
¼ t thyme
½ cup onions, chopped
¼ cup chopped olives
¼ cup chopped peppers
1 medium package natural-flavored Doritos
1 cup shredded sharp cheddar cheese
1 cup shredded Monterrey Jack cheese

Combine wheat, tomatoes, brown sugar, vinegar, soy sauce, thyme, and onions. Heat until it boils, then simmer for 1-2 hours. Pour one-half of the mixture into a casserole dish. Top with a layer of Doritos and half of the cheese. Pour on the rest of the tomato mixture. Dot with olives and peppers. Top with Doritos and the remaining cheese.

Bake at 350 degrees for 30-45 minutes.

Serves 4.

BEEF-TOMATO ORIENTAL

2 cups cooked wheat
½ cup hamburger
8-12 cherry tomatoes, peeled
½ cup water
1½ T vinegar
½ t honey
¼ t salt
2 T cornstarch
3 T soy sauce

Cook hamburger until crumbly; add cherry tomatoes and water and bring to a low boil. Gradually add vinegar, salt, honey, cornstarch, and soy sauce. Layer wheat in the bottom of a casserole dish. Top with beef-tomato mixture.

Bake at 350 degrees for 30 minutes.

Serves 4-6.

CHINESE BEEF

2 cups cooked wheat
1 t salt
2 cups boiling water
2 beef bouillon cubes
1 T soy sauce
2 chopped onions
4 stalks celery, chopped
½ cup green peppers, chopped
3 cups diced cooked beef
1 T cornstarch

Mix salt, water, bouillon cubes, soy sauce and bring to a boil. Add wheat, onion, celery, peppers and beef. Simmer 10-15 minutes. Thicken with cornstarch.

Serves 4-6.

VEGETABLE-SAUSAGE ORIENTAL

2 cups cooked wheat
1 can green beans, drained (reserve liquid)
1 can whole kernel corn, drained (reserve liquid)
4 sausage links, crisply fried and cut into pieces
2 T vinegar
14 t pepper
2 T soy sauce
1½ cups liquid from vegetables
¼ cup chopped onion
¼ cup chopped celery
2 T cornstarch

Layer cooked wheat in a casserole dish. Mix beans and corn and spoon over wheat. Blend vinegar, soy sauce, pepper, and liquid from vegetables in a sauce pan. Heat until boiling. Add sausage chunks, onion, and celery; simmer for 5 minutes before adding cornstarch. Cook until thick; spoon over vegetables.

Bake at 350 degrees for 20-30 minutes.

Serves 4-6.

VEGETABLES VINAIGRETTE

2 cups cooked wheat
2 packages frozen broccoli or French-cut green beans
¾ cup salad oil
½ t brown sugar
1 t honey
2 T chopped onion
¼ cup vinegar
2 T pickle relish

Cook vegetables until not quite done; add wheat and finish cooking. Drain. Mix remaining ingredients together and heat (do not boil). Pour over hot vegetable-wheat mixture.

Serves 6-8.

SKILLET BEANS WITH WHEAT

2 cups cooked wheat
3 strips bacon
1 can French-cut green beans, drained
1 can wax beans, drained
½ cup liquid from beans
1 t honey
2 T soy sauce

Slowly cook bacon strips; set aside. In a skillet, cook beans in 2 T bacon renderings. Mix liquid, honey, and soy sauce until smooth; add gradually to beans and simmer. Layer 1 inch of wheat in a casserole dish. Spoon bean mixture in, pouring any remaining sauce over the beans. Crumble bacon and spread on top.

Bake at 350 degrees for 15 minutes.

Serves 4.

SCALLOPED CORN

1 cup cooked wheat
¼ cup onion flakes
¼ cup water
2 cans creamed corn
¼ t black pepper American cheese slices
12 crackers, crumbled

Mix wheat, onion flakes, water. In 1½ qt. casserole dish, layer 1 can corn, ½ wheat mixture, ½ of the cracker crumbs, cover with cheese slices. Repeat, using ½ can corn, wheat, cheese, crackers, and ending with ½ can corn. Cover with cheese. Sprinkle with pepper, and cracker crumbs.

Bake at 350 degrees for 30 minutes.

Serves 4-6.

WHEAT PEAS

1 package frozen peas (10 oz.)
½ cup cooked wheat
2 cups water
2 T cornstarch 1 t soy sauce
⅛ cup onion

Bring water to a boil. Add wheat and peas and simmer until peas are tender. Combine cornstarch, soy sauce, and onion and add gradually to peas and wheat.

Serves 4.

FRENCH-ONION WHEAT

½ cup chopped onion
¼ cup butter or margarine
2 cups cooked wheat
1 can peas with liquid
2 T milk powder
2 T cornstarch

Sauté onion in butter until crisp. Add wheat and peas. Bring to a boil, set aside. Blend milk powder and cornstarch until smooth. Mix slowly into the wheat mixture. Heat through.

Serves 6-8.

STUFFED PEPPERS

4 peppers*
¼ lb. hamburger
3 cups cooked wheat
1 onion, chopped
1 can tomato paste
Salt
Pepper
Garlic powder

Brown meat, onions, and wheat. Stir in 2 Tablespoons tomato paste. Add salt, pepper; and garlic powder to taste. Stuff peppers. Pour remaining tomato paste over the top. Bake in a pan in 1½ inches of water.

Bake at 350 degrees for 2 hours.

Serves 4.

*If you want to, parboil peppers for 5 minutes. Then the baking time is cut to 40 minutes.

SEASONED MASHED POTATOES

2 cups mashed potatoes
2 T cooking oil
1 T onion flakes
½ cup *Wheat Toppers

Heat Oil. Spoon in onion flakes and mashed potatoes. Cook over high heat 3-5 minutes (until potatoes begin to crust). Fold in *Wheat Toppers.

Serves 4.

*See recipe in Sauces, Gravies, and Garnishes section.

CREAMED TUNA

1 can tuna, drained*
½ cup cooked wheat
½ cup cooked peas, drained
½ cup cooked carrots, drained (optional)
1 cup milk
2 T flour
Salt and pepper to taste

Heat milk slowly in top of a double boiler, blend in flour. Bring mixture to a boil and cook until thick. Add tuna, wheat, peas, carrots, seasoning. Heat thoroughly, stirring constantly. Serve over toast or biscuits.

Makes 6-8 cups.

*6 crisply cooked fish sticks, cut into pieces, may be substituted for the tuna.

TUNA CUPS

¼ cup chopped onion
¼ cup butter or margarine
1 can sweet peas, drained (reserve water)
2 t cornstarch
2 T melted butter
1 can tuna, drained and flaked
2 eggs
1 T lemon juice
½ t salt
¼ t pepper
1 T pickle relish
½ cup oatmeal

Sauté onions in melted butter. Stir in milk, and water from canned peas. Heat mixture to boiling, stirring constantly. Remove from heat. Blend in cornstarch and add wheat. Mix in remaining ingredients. Spoon into well-greased muffin tins. When done, turn out onto tray and serve with *Wheat-Egg Sauce.

Bake at 350 degrees for 25-30 minutes.

Serves 6 (12 cups).

*See recipe in Sauces, Gravies, and Garnishes section.

TUNA-NOODLE CASSEROLE

1 can tuna
2 cups cooked whole wheat
1 can cream of mushroom soup
1 cup milk
1 package noodles (12 oz.)
1 t salt
1 cup crumbled potato chips
2 eggs, beaten

Drain tuna. Pour hot water over tuna to clear off oil. Cook noodles in salt water until tender. Strain and mix with all ingredients except the tuna and ½ cup potato chips. Pour half of the mixture into a casserole dish. Layer with tuna and the remaining mixture. Top with potato chips.

Bake at 350 degrees for 40 minutes.

Serves 4-6.

TUNA SWEET & SOUR

1 cup pineapple tidbits
¼ cup vinegar
¼ cup brown sugar
1 T soy sauce
2 T cornstarch
1 T chopped onion
1 green pepper, sliced thin
2 tomatoes, peeled, cut into eighths
2 cans tuna
1 cup cooked wheat

Drain syrup from pineapple, mix the syrup with the vinegar and brown sugar. Combine the cornstarch with the soy sauce and add to the syrup mixture. Cook, stirring constantly, until thick. Add onion, pepper, pineapple bits, tomato wedges, and wheat. Simmer for 5 minutes. Add flaked tuna. Cook entire mixture until heated.

Bake at 350 degrees for 25 minutes.

Serves 4-6.

TUNA WHEAT

2 cups cooked whole wheat
1 can cream of mushroom soup
¼ cup milk
1 cup peas (frozen or canned)
1 can tuna
¼ cup chopped onion

Combine all ingredients in a saucepan. Stir until fully mixed. Cook, stirring constantly, until the mixture begins to boil. Serve over whole-wheat toast.

Serves 4-6.

TUNA WRAP

1 can tuna (drained)
1 cup cooked whole wheat
¼ cup diced American cheese
2 hard boiled eggs (chopped)
2 T chopped sweet pickles
2 T minced onion
4 T mayonnaise
Salt and pepper to taste

Mix all ingredients. Spread between two slices of whole wheat bread or on hamburger buns. Wrap in foil and heat.

Heat at 350 degrees for 25-30 minutes.

Serves 4-6.

SALMON NEWBURG

1 can salmon (15 oz.)
1 package frozen peas (16 oz.)
1 can cream of mushroom soup
1 can cheddar cheese soup
¼ cup chopped onion
2 cups cooked wheat
½ cup *Wheat Toppers
6 oz. sliced mushrooms (optional)
4 oz. sliced pimentos (optional)

Drain salmon; break into bite-sized pieces. Cook peas and onions, drain. Blend cheese soup with ¼ cup water. Layer wheat, salmon, peas, mushrooms and pimentos, and cheese soup in a casserole dish. Pour cream of mushroom soup over the top. Chill. Before baking, sprinkle with *Wheat Toppers.

Bake uncovered at 350 degrees for 80 minutes.

Serves 4.

*See recipe in Sauces, Gravies, and Garnishes section.

MACKEREL PIE

2 T margarine
2 T flour
¼ cup evaporated milk
1 can peas drained, (reserve water)
½ t grated lemon rind
¼ t pepper
1 t salt
1 can mackerel drained (1 lb.) (reserve oil)
2 cups cooked wheat

Melt the margarine and blend with flour. Remove from heat and stir in milk diluted with liquid from the peas. Cook slowly until thick. Add lemon rind, seasonings, liquid from mackerel, peas, and wheat. Place mackerel into a 2-qt. casserole dish. Pour sauce over fish.

Bake at 425 degrees for 15 minutes.

Serves 2-4.

MACKEREL RING

1 egg
1 can mackerel drained (16 oz.)
1 cup cooked wheat
½ cup chopped onion
½ cup shredded cheese
½ cup parsley
1 T celery, finely chopped
¼ t pepper
½ cup frozen broccoli cuts
3 cups flour
½ cup shortening
4 t baking powder
¼ t salt
1 cup milk

Beat egg slightly. Reserve 2 tablespoons. Stir onion, mackerel, wheat, cheese, parsley, celery, pepper, broccoli into remaining egg. Set aside.

Mix flour, shortening, baking powder, salt and milk. Knead slightly, then roll into 15-inch by 10-inch rectangle. Spread with mackerel mixture. Roll, beginning with the long side. Shape into a ring on a greased cookie sheet. Pinch ends. Cut at one-inch intervals, ⅔ of the way through. Brush the top with egg. Serve with cheese sauce.

Bake at 375 degrees for 25-30 minutes.

Serves 4-6.

TUNA LOAF

¼ cup chopped onion
¼ cup butter or margarine
¾ cup milk
1 cup cooked wheat (or cracked wheat)
½ cup oatmeal
2 cans tuna, drained and flaked
2 eggs
1 T lemon juice
½ t salt
¼ t pepper
1 T pickle relish
*Wheat-Egg Sauce

Sauté onion in butter, stir in milk, heat to boiling. Remove from heat, blend in wheat, then add remaining ingredients. Pour into greased 9x5x3-inch pan. Serve with *Wheat-Egg Sauce.

Bake at 375 degrees for 45 minutes.

Serves 6.

*See recipe in Sauces, Gravies, and Garnishes section.

CHICKEN CACCIATORE

2 cups cooked wheat
2 cups chicken, cut into bite-sized pieces
½ cup flour
1 t salt
¼ t pepper
3 T oil
¼ cup chopped onion
1 garlic clove, chopped
1 can tomatoes (16 oz.)
1 t honey
½ t basil
¼ t thyme
1 medium green pepper, sliced

Coat chicken with flour, salt, and pepper. Sauté pieces in oil. Remove. Sauté onion and garlic. Add tomatoes, basil, honey, and thyme. Add chicken pieces. Pour wheat into casserole dish. Top with chicken and sauce, garnish with pepper slices.

Bake at 350 degrees for 45 minutes.

Serves 4-6.

CHICKEN ORIENTAL

4 chicken breasts
1 t salt
2 packages frozen peas (or peas with water chestnuts)
2 cups cooked wheat
3 T cider vinegar
¼ t pepper
2 T cornstarch
3 T soy sauce

Remove skin from chicken. Cut the meat from the bones, then slice into ¼ inch strips. Sauté the chicken in a frying pan with the salt. Set aside.

Cook the peas in a frying pan until thawed, adding ¼ cup water if needed. Add vinegar and pepper to the peas. Mix together the soy sauce and cornstarch (with 2 T water), and add to peas. Stir in chicken pieces and cook until thick.

Layer 1 inch wheat in a casserole dish, spoon chicken mixture on top. Chill for one hour.

Bake at 350 degrees for 30 minutes.

Serves 4.

CHICKEN DIVAN

2 cups cooked wheat
2 cups cooked chicken
2 packages (10 oz.) broccoli spears
6 slices cheese
1 can evaporated milk
1 can cream of mushroom soup (undiluted)
1 can prepared French-fried onion rings

Layer wheat and chicken in a casserole dish. Top with hot broccoli. Cover with cheese. Stir milk and soup together and pour over the cheese slices. Bake 25 minutes. Lay onion rings on top and bake 5 minutes longer.

Bake at 350 degrees for 25 minutes covered, then 5 minutes uncovered.

Serves 4.

WHEAT-CRUNCH CHICKEN

1 chicken, cut-up for baking
1 cup medium-coarse whole wheat flour
1 t salt
¼ t pepper
2 T paprika
½ cup shortening (part butter or margarine)

Put shortening in a 9 x 13-inch pan to melt. Mix dry ingredients together in a paper bag. Place the chicken pieces in the bag, and shake. Lay chicken pieces in pan and bake for 45 minutes. Turn each piece and cook 15 minutes more. Any remaining flour mixture may be sprinkled over the chicken as it bakes.

Bake at 425 degrees for 60 minutes, turn each piece at last 15 minutes of baking time.

Serves 4-6.

VOLCANOES

1 can corned beef hash (16 oz.)
2 cups cooked wheat
2 eggs
4 cups mashed potatoes
1 cup shredded cheese
½ cup tomato sauce

Mix hash, wheat, and eggs. Form ½ cup at a time into mounds. Bake at 350 degrees for 15 minutes. Frost lightly with mashed potatoes. Top with cheese. Bake until cheese melts. Dribble tomato sauce over the top and heat.

Serves 4.

TACO SALAD

½ lb. hamburger
2 cups cooked wheat
½ medium onion, diced
1 avocado
½ head lettuce
3 medium tomatoes
½ cup grated cheese
1 can tomato sauce

Sauté hamburger and onion, adding seasonings (salt, pepper, garlic, cumin) to taste. Drain excess grease, add wheat and tomato sauce. Dice avocado and tear lettuce. Slice tomatoes and toss with lettuce and avocado. Add hamburger mixture and toss. Garnish with cheese. Serve over tortilla chips with hot sauce.

Serves 4-6.

ONION-WHEAT SPOONBURGERS

½ lb. hamburger
2 cups cooked wheat
2 T whole wheat flour
salt to taste
1 can condensed onion soup

Brown hamburger and add wheat. Sprinkle in flour, stir until thoroughly mixed. Add onion soup. Cook until heated and slightly thick. Salt to taste. Spoon on bread slices or hamburger buns.

Serves 4-6.

SLOPPY FRANKS

2 frankfurters, finely chopped
1 cup cooked wheat
¼ cup bacon crumbs
1 can tomato sauce
1 t prepared mustard
1 T pickle relish
1 boiled egg, finely chopped
½ cup grated cheese
Hotdog buns

Fry the bacon, add hot dogs and wheat and heat thoroughly. Stir in tomato sauce, mustard, relish, egg, and cheese. Spoon onto hot dog buns.

Serves 6.

CORNMEAL TACOS

½ lb. hamburger
3 cups cooked wheat
1 can tomatoes
1 cup catsup
¼ cup packed brown sugar
2 T vinegar
2 T soy sauce
1 t salt
1 envelope onion soup mix
3 eggs
1½ cups milk
1 cup whole wheat flour
1 t salt
½ cup cornmeal
2 T melted butter
1 can tomato paste
1 cup shredded cheese
½ cup cubed green pepper

Brown hamburger; add ingredients down to and including onion soup mix. Simmer for 2 hours. Combine eggs, milk, flour, salt, cornmeal, and butter into a pancake mix. Pour ¼ cup into a 7-inch pan and fry as crepes (makes 12). Spoon ¼ cup meat sauce on each pancake, roll, and place seam side down in a baking pan. Pour on tomato paste, cheese, and green pepper topping.

Bake at 350 degrees for 25 minutes.

Serves 6.

CHEESE ROULADEN

4 thin slices of beef
prepared mustard
½ t rosemary
½ t salt
¼ t pepper
½ cup onion, chopped
1 cup shredded cheese
½ cup cooked wheat
2 T oil
2 T soy sauce
2 T cornstarch
½ cup milk

Spread mustard thinly on each slice of beef.

Mix seasonings, onion, cheese, and wheat in a small bowl; spoon evenly on each slice of beef. Roll the slices and pin edges with toothpicks (making sure that the filling does not spill out). Brown the rolls in hot oil. When brown, add the soy sauce. Fill skillet to 1 inch with water and bring to a boil. Cover. Simmer for 75 minutes, adding water if necessary.

After the rolls are removed, add cornstarch and milk to remaining water and heat to boil for gravy.

Serves 4.

SWEET WHEAT

1 lb. hamburger
1 cup soaked raisins
1 medium apple, peeled and diced
1 can pineapple chunks (16 oz.)
2 T cornstarch
2 T water
2 cups cooked wheat

Fry hamburger over slow heat; drain. Mix raisins, diced apple, pineapple (with juice) with hamburger and cook until apple softens. Blend water and cornstarch and mix into meat mixture. Add wheat (and water, if needed). Simmer 15 minutes to allow the flavors to mix. Serve with vegetables or salad.

Serves 4.

SLOPPY JOES

½ lb. hamburger
2 cups cooked wheat
1 onion, diced
1 bell pepper, diced
2 cups tomato soup, undiluted
Chili powder to taste
1 cup grated cheese

Cook hamburger and wheat, drain. Add remaining ingredients, except cheese. Simmer ½ hour, or until the pepper is done. Add cheese. Spoon onto hamburger buns or whole-wheat bread and heat under broiler 5 minutes.

Serves 6.

GLAZED PORK CHOPS

4 pork chops
1 onion, cut into rings
½ cup brown sugar
½ t salt
1 cup cooked wheat

Cut fat from the chops. Render part of the fat into grease. Cook the chops on both sides until brown. Pour off excess fat. Sprinkle ½ of the brown sugar and salt over the chops. Layer onion rings on top. Sprinkle a thin layer of wheat, then the remainder of the brown sugar and salt. Cover loosely and heat on low for 45 minutes.

Serves 4.

HAMBURG BUTTERMILK SOUP

2 cups milk
½ cup honey
Pinch salt
2 T butter or margarine
Lemon peel
½ small box Cream of Wheat
1 egg
1 qt. buttermilk
Lemon peel
½ cup honey
1 t cinnamon
3 T cornstarch
3 T water
1 qt. soaked mixed dried fruit, drained
1 T lemon juice
2 cups smoked sausage bits
1 cup cooked wheat

Mix milk, honey, salt, butter and lemon peel in a medium saucepan. Heat to boiling. Gradually add Cream of Wheat until mixture is thick and pulls away from the sides of the pan. Stir in egg.

In another pan, mix together buttermilk, lemon peel, honey, cinnamon and heat slowly. Before the mixture boils, add the cornstarch blended with the water. Bring to a boil.

Drop Cream of Wheat dumplings from a wet spoon into the buttermilk, removing lemon peel. Stir in mixed fruit and allow to simmer 15 minutes. Then add smoked sausage bits and whole wheat. Heat on low another hour, stirring occasionally and adding water if necessary. Serve hot.

Serves 6-8.

WHEAT LOAF

½ lb. hamburger
2 cups cooked wheat
2 T melted butter
2 eggs, beaten slightly
2 T chopped onion
1 t salt
¼ t pepper
½ cup oatmeal (or crushed crackers)
¾ cup milk
1 T prepared mustard
2 T catsup

Combine all ingredients. Form into loaf on greased cookie· sheet, or press into greased and floured loaf pan. Bake for 1 hour, then garnish (with tomato sauce, cheese, bacon strips, green peppers, or tomato slices). Bake ½ hour longer.

Bake at 375 degrees for 1½ hours.

Serves 4.

BARBECUED WHEAT LOAF

1 lb. hamburger
2 cups cooked wheat
1 cup bread crumbs
1 onion, finely chopped
1 egg
1½ t salt
¼ t pepper
½ cup water
2 cans tomato sauce
3 T vinegar
1½ T honey
2 t prepared mustard

Combine hamburger, wheat, bread crumbs, onion, egg, salt, pepper, and 1 can tomato sauce. Form into loaf. Mix remaining sauce, water, vinegar, honey, and mustard, and pour over loaf.

Bake at 350 degrees for 75 minutes.

Serves 4-6.

CHI CHOW

2 cups beef cut in thin strips
2 T oil
¼ cup onion
¼ cup celery
½ cup wheat sprouts
1 cup sliced mushrooms
1 cup water
1 can peaches, drained
2 T cornstarch
¼ cup soy sauce
2 cups cooked wheat
¼ t ginger

Sauté onion and celery. Add beef and mushrooms. Add 1 cup water, soy sauce, and cornstarch. Add drained peaches and wheat sprouts. Mix together the wheat and ginger, then layer mixture in the bottom of a casserole dish. Spoon on beef mixture.

Bake at 350 degrees for 15 minutes.

Serves 4-6.

HAM-'N'-BROCCOLI

1 package frozen broccoli, cut into pieces
3 T butter or margarine
2 T diced onion
3 T flour
½ t salt
Pepper to taste
1½ cups milk
1½ cups diced ham
2 cups cooked wheat

Cook broccoli; drain. Sauté onion in butter. Stir in flour, salt, pepper, and milk. Cook until sauce thickens and bubbles 1 minute. Stir in ham, broccoli, and wheat.

Serve over toast.

HAM-'N'-PINEAPPLE

1 cup ham, cut into thin strips
1 can pineapple (with liquid)
¼ cup celery
1 cup water
2 cups cooked wheat
2 T soy sauce
2 T cornstarch

Cook ham strips. Add pineapple, celery, water, soy sauce and simmer for 10 minutes. Thicken with cornstarch. Spoon wheat into the bottom of a 1-qt. casserole dish. Top with ham-pineapple mixture.

Bake at 350 degrees for 30 minutes.

Serves 4-6.

VEGETABLE CROWN IMPERIAL

½ lb. hamburger
2 cups cooked wheat
2 eggs
¼ cup whole wheat flour
½ onion, chopped
1 can Veg-All, drained
3 cups prepared mashed potatoes
2 cups brown gravy
Peach slices
Seasonings to taste

Line a ring pan with shortening and coarsely ground whole wheat flour. Combine hamburger, wheat, eggs, wheat flour, onion, seasonings, and Veg-All as if for a meat loaf. Form in ring pan and bake. Bake at 400 degrees for 30 minutes

Turn the ring loaf out on a serving platter and fill the center with mashed potatoes.

Arrange peach slices around the mashed potatoes, then top with brown gravy.

Serve immediately.

Serves 8.

HOBO GOULASH

¼ lb. hamburger
2 cups cooked wheat
1 large can stewed tomatoes
½ cup chopped onion
2 cups prepared macaroni and cheese
¼ t thyme
¼ t ground sage
¼ t garlic salt
¼ t ground black pepper

Brown the hamburger in a large skillet. Add wheat, tomatoes, onion, and macaroni and cheese. Simmer. Add spices. Simmer on low heat for 15 minutes.

Serves 4-6.

PATCHWORK CASSEROLE

1 cup cooked whole wheat
1 medium green pepper, chopped
1 small onion, chopped
3 cups corn (canned, drained; or frozen)
1 t salt
¼ t pepper
2 medium tomatoes, cut into wedges

Sauté green pepper and onion in butter or margarine. Add corn, wheat, salt, and pepper. Cook over low heat 10-12 minutes. Add tomato wedges and simmer 5-10 minutes more.

Serves 6.

SOUP-'N'-SANDWICHES

TOMATO-WHEAT SOUP

1 can tomato soup
¼ cup grated sharp cheese
1 cup milk
1 T onion flakes
1 cup cooked wheat
1 can stewed tomatoes, drained

Blend soup and milk thoroughly. As soup is heated (over low heat), stir in grated cheese and onion flakes. Bring to a gentle boil, stirring constantly. Add cooked wheat and stewed tomatoes. Simmer 15 minutes. Add black pepper to taste.

Serves 4.

BLT WHEAT

½ cup whole wheat
2 slices bacon, cut into 1-inch pieces
¼ t garlic flakes
¼ t onion salt
Sliced tomatoes
Lettuce

Fry bacon pieces slowly until crisp. Remove reserving oil. Fry wheat in bacon grease. Season with onion salt and garlic flakes. Layer lettuce, tomato slices, and wheat on whole wheat bread. Garnish with bacon crumbs.

BACON-BEEF GRINDER

¼ cup bacon crumbs
½ cup hamburger
½ cup cooked wheat
¼ cup onion, chopped and sautéed
¼ cup grated cheddar cheese
2 sourdough rolls, split
Lettuce
Salt and pepper to taste
¼ cup *Wheat Toppers

Fry bacon, set aside. Fry hamburger and wheat in bacon renderings. Layer onion, hamburger-wheat, bacon crumbs, *Wheat Toppers, cheese, and shredded lettuce on two sourdough roll halves. Cover with remaining roll halves. Wrap in foil.

Bake at 350 degrees for 10 minutes.

Serves 2.

*See recipe in Sauces, Gravies, and Garnishes section.

BARBECUED CHEESE-'N'-WHEAT

1½ cups diced American cheese
3 hard boiled eggs, diced
1½ t onion, grated
½ cup evaporated milk
3 T catsup
¼ t pepper
½ t salt
½ cup cooked wheat
2 t pickle relish (optional)

Combine all ingredients in large mixing bowl. Arrange ¼ cup on split hamburger buns or whole wheat bread.

Bake at 400 degrees for 7 minutes, or until the cheese melts.

Serves 6.

SUNDAY NIGHT QUICK-SNACK

4 eggs
½ cup cooked wheat
1 can cream of chicken soup (undiluted)
½ T chopped onion.

Beat eggs slightly; add soup, wheat and onion. Pour into buttered skillet and scramble. Serve on hot toast.

Serves 2-3.

TUNA SNACK

1 can tuna, drained and flaked
¼ cup cooked whole wheat
2 T sweet pickle relish
1 T lemon juice

Mix first three ingredients in a small bowl.

Sprinkle generously with lemon juice. Chill and serve.

WHEAT-EGG SANDWICH

3 eggs, hard-boiled
½ cup mayonnaise or salad dressing
¼ cup diced pickles
½ cup cooked whole wheat
Salt and pepper to taste
¼ cup vinegar from pickles

Chop boiled eggs finely. In a small bowl, mix all ingredients thoroughly. Spread on thin slices of whole-wheat bread.

DESSERTS

APPLE-MARSHMALLOW TREAT

1 cup cooked wheat
2 cups marshmallow bits
1 t cinnamon
5 apples, sliced
2 cups water
¼ cup honey
1 t cinnamon
2 t cornstarch

Boil wheat 15 minutes. Melt marshmallows in the top of a double boiler; stir in wheat and cinnamon. Press in the bottom of a small casserole dish. Cook the remaining ingredients in a small saucepan, stirring until they thicken. Pour over the wheat-marshmallow mixture.

Bake at 350 degrees for 15 minutes.

Serves 6-8.

FRUIT COMPOTE

1 can pineapple chunks
1 can peach slices
1 can apricot halves
1 cup raisins (soaked)
½ cup water
2 cooked apples, diced
⅛ cup honey
¼ cup *Cinnamon Nuts
1 T lemon juice

Drain fruit, reserving pineapple juice and ½ cup apricot juice. Mix pineapple and apricot juice, honey and lemon juice. Heat until bubbly. Stir in fruit and *Cinnamon Nuts. Heat thoroughly.

Serves 4-6.

*See recipe in Sauces, Gravies, and Garnishes section.

BREAKFASTS

BREAKFAST BARS

1 cup peanut butter
½ cup honey
¼ cup butter or margarine
1½ cups whole wheat flour
½ cup milk powder
1 cup cooked wheat
1 cup raisins
½ cup oatmeal
½ cup chocolate chips
¼ cup coconut

Combine all ingredients and bake in a greased 9-inch by 9-inch pan. Cook. Cut in to 1 inch by 1½ inch bars.

Bake at 350 degrees for 35-40 minutes.

INSTANT BREAKFAST

4 fruit yogurts
½ cup cubed cheese
1 medium apple, cubed
¼ cup raisins (soaked)
¼ cup cooked whole wheat
¼ cup oatmeal (optional)

Spoon each yogurt into a shallow bowl. Mix remaining ingredients, then divide evenly among four bowls, spooning over the top of the yogurts. Serve cold.

Serves 4.

SAUCES
GRAVIES
GARNISHES

BEEF GRAVY

2 cup chuck steak, cut into small pieces
1 cup cooked wheat
1 can cream of mushroom soup, undiluted
1 cup milk
Pepper
Salt
1 t garlic flakes

Fry the meat, then add wheat, mushroom soup and milk. Simmer, stirring constantly. Serve with mashed potatoes.

SPAGHETTI-WHEAT SAUCE

¼ lb. hamburger
2 small cans tomato paste
2 cups cooked wheat
¼ onion, chopped
1 qt. drained stewed tomatoes
1 clove garlic
1 small bell pepper, diced (optional)
½ t oregano ,
Salt and pepper to taste

Combine all ingredients in a large saucepan.

Bring to a boil, stirring constantly, then simmer on low heat at least an hour.

WHEAT-EGG SAUCE

1 T onion
3 T butter or margarine
3 T whole wheat flour
3 eggs, boiled and diced
½ t salt
¼ t pepper
1½ cups milk
¼ cup cooked wheat

Sauté onions in butter; blend in flour, salt, pepper, and milk. Heat until smooth and thick. Add egg and cooked wheat.

PEACH WAFFLE SAUCE

2 cups canned peaches
¼ cup *Cinnamon Nuts
1 T cornstarch

Mix all ingredients thoroughly. Heat until boiling, then simmer until thick. Serve over whole wheat waffles.

*See recipe below.

CINNAMON NUTS

¼ cup wheat
½ cup water
1 t cinnamon (or 1 stick)

Boil wheat in water for 15 minutes. Add cinnamon, boil 5 minutes longer. Let stand for 20 minutes, drain.

WHEAT STUFFING

4 cups dried, crumbled cornbread
½ cup butter or margarine
½ t salt
½ t pepper
1 cup cooked wheat
Whole leaf sage to taste
1 medium onion, diced
¼ cup celery (optional)
1 to 1½ cup boiling water

Mix together all ingredients except boiling water. Add just enough water to moisten stuffing thoroughly.

Stuffs a 10-14 lb. turkey.

WHEAT TOPPERS

½ cup cooked wheat
½ t garlic flakes
Salt to taste
2 T oil

Mix all ingredients thoroughly. Layer one-kernel deep on cookie sheet. Toast under high heat (500 degrees) until wheat crisps, browns, and pops. Stir occasionally.

NUT WHEAT

¼ cup wheat
½ cup water
½ t nut flavoring (almond, walnut, pecan, etc.)

Boil wheat in water and flavoring 5 minutes (don't allow the wheat to boil dry). Set aside for 10 minutes. Drain.

Use in place of walnuts, blanched almonds, etc.

AFTERWORD
ON LIVING WITH WHEAT

UNGROUND WHOLE WHEAT entered my life early, although at the time I did not appreciate its potentials.

When I was a child, my family spent most of our vacations at my grandfather's dry farm in the mountains of southeast Idaho. Because of my father's schedule, we were usually there during the final weeks of summer…generally after the grain harvest was finished.

In addition to the usual huge round metal storage building, my grandfather had a small old pioneer granary that was part of a string of outbuildings (including his machine shop, an open garage, and much farther down, a highly sophisticated four-hole outhouse that was still in use into the 1960s) along the path of a small creek that bisected his farm. As with all of them, he had built the low-slung granary himself of logs, now worn by time to silver-gray, with hand-split shingles, no windows, and a low door hung on hinges he had forged himself during the 1940s. Unlike the other buildings, the granary was raised a foot or so off the ground, presumably to discourage rodents and other vermin that might otherwise come calling for a free meal.

Inside, the floor was composed of close-set wooden planks, originally unfinished but worn by time into a satin-like patina. The wheat was stored along the far wall, a huge pile of it that spilled down toward the door.

One day my mother and I were inside for some reason. I remember the warm, dense smell of the wheat, the feeling that everything was dusty and time-worn. She reached down and lifted a handful of kernels.

"We used to chew this," she said, giving me a few grains. "It was like chewing gum for us."

I tried it.

I was not impressed. Perhaps my young taste buds had already been jaded by the intense flavor and moisture of Juicy Fruit and Dentine, the only brands my mother would buy.

I told her so.

"Well, it was either wheat or small wads of pine sap picked right off the trees. We didn't have the money to waste on store-bought gum back then."

Given the alternative, perhaps the wheat was not so bad.

After that, whole wheat and I went our separate ways for almost two decades. By the time we met again, I was a graduate student in English literature, married, and trying to support a wife and two babies on my stipend from the university and Judi's income selling cosmetics door-to-door. A friend offered me a part time job in her bookstore/food storage outlet at the princely sum of $2.00 an hours.

Considering the fact that my monthly income from teaching was about $125, and that our two bedroom married-students' house (a holdover from a World-War II army officers' quarters complex snapped up by the university when the army base closed some years before) was just under $100, the job was a life-saver.

Before long, a fair amount of my hourly wages was being invested in foodstuffs: dehydrated fruits and vegetables that the kids could chew on like candy and that became staples in Judi's cooking; canisters of dried milk; flavored soy proteins (new on the market and, while not particularly appetizing, rich in nutriments); and…unground wheat.

We bought it in plastic tubs designed for long-term storage, since that was the least expensive way. Initially, we purchased wheat in five-gallon buckets, then later augmented those with large Tupperware containers when Judi began selling for the company. It didn't take long to realize that we had a serious problem.

Married-student housing, and afterward the apartment we rented, offered almost no storage. Buckets of wheat began taking up space under the babies' cribs, behind furniture, along otherwise unused walls. It became, to say the least, cumbersome.

Then…the flash of inspiration.

First, the master-bed went. Instead, we carefully stacked the Tupperware canisters in rows, since they were all the same height. Over them came one-half-inch plywood sheets, and over that our old mattress. And *voilà!*—instant space for food storage.

Next, as our oldest child graduated from the crib and our third took his place there, we constructed a special three-foot-by-four-foot plywood frame, about three inches taller than the Tupperware canisters, with a hinged drop-leaf to cover the containers. Add a similar-sized four-inch-thick foam-rubber sheet for a mattress…and we had a child's-bed-*cum*-food-storage unit. Eventually, we built four of these beds. They gave the children additional floor space for playing and served well for sleeping until we finally gave in and bought full-sized beds (when both the children and our budget grew large enough).

Finally, we took the plunge, and wheat invaded the living room. The old sofa we had inherited from friends at the university, probably at least fifth-hand, finally gave out. In its place we built—you guessed it—a sofa-sized frame of three-quarters-inch plywood, tastefully edged with floral molding and stained dark oak to match the antique sideboard that was our one piece of real "furniture." Into it we placed the five-gallon buckets of wheat (as well as several containing rice, salt, boxes of macaroni and cheese, and other long-term staples). Then came the four-inch sheet of foam rubber, encased in a cheerful autumn-print cotton case, and several throw pillows, and our sofa was finished. To complete the set, we made an arm-chair as well. Matching end tables were provided by two five-gallon buckets of wheat topped by twenty-four-inch plywood rounds, each covered by floor-length cloths of the same material we had used on the sofa and chair.

That living room suite followed us around, by the way, for almost fifteen years, when Judi's parents retired one of their sofas and donated it to the cause of making the Collings household seem slightly less idiosyncratic.

Eventually, though, we were able to keep all of our stored wheat out of sight…but not out of mind.

Through all this time, we not only slept on wheat and sat on wheat…but we *ate* wheat as well. Judi would crank the hand-grinder out on the back porch to make fresh whole-wheat flour for pancakes, waffles, and bread; eventually we could afford a small electric mill and used one of the Tupperware canisters to store a week's worth of flour at a time.

We began incorporating unground, cooked whole wheat into our daily meals as well. It began simply enough. A cup of wheat, boiled in about two-thirds cup of water and left to sit overnight, actually made a tasty exchange for hot oatmeal as a breakfast cereal when heated up the next morning. From there, it was but a small step to tossing a handful of cooked wheat into scrambled eggs. Then the serious experiments began.

Eating that much wheat made for occasionally interesting diaper changes for the children as they neared the end of their potty-training, but on the whole they took to the regimen well enough. All of the recipes in *Whole Wheat for Food Storage*, and more, found themselves on our table at least once. In several instances, they became either staples or recurring fancy-dinner treats. The children were free at any time to make their responses known; on one unforgettable—and disastrous—evening, we had dabbled in a casserole featuring Vienna sausages.

That was the first and only time the family decided, by unanimous vote—that the dish properly belonged in the garbage and the humans tasting it even more properly belonged at McDonalds! So there we went.

We kept to this program for a number of years. The result was one of our first publications, *Whole Wheat Harvest: Recipes for Unground Wheat* (Hawkes, 1980). My first book with Hawkes, a collection of LDS poetry called *A Season of Calm Weather* (1974; now incorporated in *Tales Through Time: Selected Poems*, Borgo Press, 2010) had paid the hospital expenses for the birth of our first son.

Whole Wheat Harvest, and indeed whole wheat itself, helped keep food on the table for him, his three subsequent siblings, Judi, and me for some years to come.

It took time, but at last I began to understand the potentials of living with and eating unground whole wheat.

NOTES AND PERSONAL RECIPES

A GLANCE THROUGH the pages of *Whole Wheat for Food Storage* should make it clear that none—or at least few—of the recipes included are startlingly original. Most are simply takes on foods that our family had always enjoyed, modified to incorporate unground whole wheat.

It took a bit of trial and error to discover which combinations worked and which did not, which textures tasted better when mixed with unground wheat and which did not. The successes made their way into this book; the failures...well, occasionally they did not even make their way off the stove top.

In that spirit of adventure and experimentation, we invite you to apply some of the same techniques to your favorite dishes. The following pages are left intentionally blank so you may record your results.

Have fun!—and *Bon Appétit*.

NOTES AND PERSONAL RECIPES

NOTES AND PERSONAL RECIPES

NOTES AND PERSONAL RECIPES

NOTES AND PERSONAL RECIPES

NOTES AND PERSONAL RECIPES

INDEX TO RECIPES BY NAME

Apple-Marshmallow Treat, 87
Bacon-Beef Grinder, 79
Barbecued Cheese-'n'-Wheat, 80
Barbecued Wheat Loaf, 66
Beef Gravy, 95
Beef-Tomato Oriental, 25
BLT Wheat, 78
Breakfast Bars, 91
Button Casserole, 20
Cheese Rouladen, 58
Chi Chow, 67
Chicken Cacciatore, 47
Chicken Divan, 50
Chinese Beef, 26
Cinnamon Nuts, 99
Cornmeal Tacos, 56
Creamed Tuna, 35
Doritos Bake, 23
Five-Layer Bake, 18
French-Onion Wheat, 32
Fruit Compote, 88

Garden Casserole, 13
Glazed Pork Chops, 62
Ham-'n'-Broccoli, 68
Ham-'n'-Pineapple, 69
Hamburg Buttermilk Soup, 63
Hobo Goulash, 72
Instant Breakfast, 92
Kraut Casserole, 15
Lasagna, 21
Mackerel Pie, 43
Mackerel Ring, 44
Nut Wheat, 102
Onion-Wheat Spoonburgers, 54
Patchwork Casserole, 73
Peach Waffle Sauce, 98
Rainy-Day Picnic Casserole, 17
Salmon Newburg, 42
Sausage Casserole, 16
Sausage-'n'-Onions, 19
Scalloped Corn, 30
Seasoned Mashed Potatoes, 34
Skillet Beans with Wheat, 29
Sloppy Franks, 55
Sloppy Joes, 61
Spaghetti-Wheat Sauce, 96
Stuffed Peppers, 33
Sunday Night Quick-Snack, 81
Sweet Wheat, 60
Taco Salad, 53
Tomato-Wheat Soup, 77

Tuna Cups, 36
Tuna Loaf, 46
Tuna Snack, 82
Tuna Sweet & Sour, 39
Tuna Wheat, 40
Tuna Wrap, 41
Tuna-Noodle Casserole, 38
Vegetable Crown Imperial, 70
Vegetables Vinaigrette, 28
Vegetable-Sausage Oriental, 27
Volcanoes, 52
Wheat Loaf, 65
Wheat Peas, 31
Wheat Stuffing, 100
Wheat Toppers, 101
Wheat-Crunch Chicken, 51
Wheat-Egg Sandwich, 83
Wheat-Egg Sauce, 97

INDEX TO RECIPES BY COURSES

BREAKFASTS, 89
Breakfast Bars, 91
Instant Breakfast, 92

DESSERTS, 85
Apple-Marshmallow Treat, 87
Fruit Compote, 88

MAIN COURSES, 11
Barbecued Wheat Loaf, 66
Beef-Tomato Oriental, 25
Button Casserole, 20
Cheese Rouladen, 58
Chi Chow, 67
Chicken Cacciatore, 47
Chicken Divan, 50
Chicken Oriental, 48
Chinese Beef, 26
Cornmeal Tacos, 56
Creamed Tuna, 35
Doritos Bake, 23

Five-Layer Bake, 18
French-Onion Wheat, 32
Garden Casserole, 13
Glazed Pork Chops, 62
Ham-'n'-Broccoli, 68
Ham-'n'-Pineapple, 69
Hamburg Buttermilk Soup, 63
Hobo Goulash, 72
Kraut Casserole, 15
Lasagna, 21
Mackerel Pie, 43
Mackerel Ring, 44
Onion-Wheat Spoonburgers, 54
Patchwork Casserole, 73
Rainy-Day Picnic Casserole, 17
Salmon Newburg, 42
Sausage Casserole, 16
Sausage-'n'-Onions, 19
Scalloped Corn, 30
Seasoned Mashed Potatoes, 34
Skillet Beans with Wheat, 29
Sloppy Franks, 55
Sloppy Joes, 61
Stuffed Peppers, 33
Sweet Wheat, 60
Taco Salad, 53
Tuna Cups, 36
Tuna Loaf, 46
Tuna Sweet & Sour, 39
Tuna Wheat, 40

Tuna Wrap, 41
Tuna-Noodle Casserole, 38
Vegetable Crown Imperial, 70
Vegetables Vinaigrette, 28
Vegetable-Sausage Oriental, 27
Volcanoes, 52
Wheat Loaf, 65
Wheat Peas, 31
Wheat-Crunch Chicken, 51

SAUCES-GRAVIES-GARNISHES, 93
Beef Gravy, 95
Cinnamon Nuts, 99
Nut Wheat, 102
Peach Waffle Sauce, 98
Spaghetti-Wheat Sauce, 96
Wheat Stuffing, 100
Wheat Toppers, 101
Wheat-Egg Sauce, 97

SOUP-'N'-SANDWICHES, 75
Bacon-Beef Grinder, 79
Barbecued Cheese-'n'-Wheat, 80
BLT Wheat, 78
Sunday Night Quick-Snack, 81
Tomato-Wheat Soup, 77
Tuna Snack, 82
Wheat-Egg Sandwich, 83

INDEX TO RECIPES BY PRIMARY FOOD GROUPS

FISH
Creamed Tuna, 35
Mackerel Pie, 43
Mackerel Ring, 44
Salmon Newburg, 42
Tuna Cups, 36
Tuna Loaf, 46
Tuna Snack, 82
Tuna Sweet & Sour, 39
Tuna Wrap, 41
Tuna-Noodle Casserole, 38

FRUIT
Apple-Marshmallow Treat, 87
Breakfast Bars, 91
Fruit Compote, 88
Ham-'n'-Pineapple, 69
Hamburg Buttermilk Soup, 63
Instant Breakfast, 92
Peach Waffle Sauce, 98
Taco Salad, 53

Tuna Sweet & Sour, 39

MEATS—BEEF, PORK, SAUSAGE, & OTHERS

BEEF, HAMBURGER, CORNED BEEF HASH
Bacon-Beef Grinder, 79
Barbecued Wheat Loaf, 66
Beef Gravy, 95
Beef-Tomato Oriental, 25
Cheese Rouladen, 58
Chi Chow, 67
Chinese Beef, 26
Cornmeal Tacos, 56
Five-Layer Bake, 18
Hobo Goulash, 72
Onion-Wheat Spoonburgers, 54
Sloppy Joes, 61
Spaghetti-Wheat Sauce, 96
Stuffed Peppers, 33
Sweet Wheat, 60
Taco Salad, 53
Vegetable Crown Imperial, 70
Volcanoes, 52
Wheat Loaf, 65

PORK, BACON, SAUSAGE, FRANKFURTERS
Bacon-Beef Grinder, 79
BLT Wheat, 78
Button Casserole, 20
Glazed Pork Chops, 62
Ham-'n'-Broccoli, 68

Ham-'n'-Pineapple, 69
Hamburg Buttermilk Soup, 63
Lasagna, 21
Rainy-Day Picnic Casserole, 17
Sausage Casserole, 16
Sausage-'n'-Onions, 19
Skillet Beans with Wheat, 29
Sloppy Franks, 55
Vegetable-Sausage Oriental, 27

PASTA
Hobo Goulash, 72
Lasagna, 21
Tuna-Noodle Casserole, 38

POULTRY—CHICKEN AND EGGS
Barbecued Cheese-'n'-Wheat, 80
Chicken Cacciatore, 47
Chicken Divan, 50
Chicken Oriental, 48
Wheat-Crunch Chicken, 51
Wheat-Egg Sandwich, 83
Wheat-Egg Sauce, 97

SOUP
Five-Layer Bake, 18
Sunday Night Quick-Snack, 81
Tomato-Wheat Soup, 77

VEGETABLES
Beef-Tomato Oriental, 25

Button Casserole, 20
Chicken Oriental, 48
Cooked Wheat
Doritos Bake, 23
Five-Layer Bake, 18
Garden Casserole, 13
Ham-'n'-Broccoli, 68
Kraut Casserole, 15
Mackerel Pie, 43
Patchwork Casserole, 73
Rainy-Day Picnic Casserole, 17
Salmon Newburg, 42
Sausage-'n'-Onions, 19
Scalloped Corn, 30
Seasoned Mashed Potatoes, 34
Skillet Beans with Wheat, 29
Stuffed Peppers, 33
Tuna Wheat, 40
Vegetable Crown Imperial, 70
Vegetables Vinaigrette, 28
Vegetable-Sausage Oriental, 27
Wheat Peas, 31
Wheat-Crunch Chicken, 51

ABOUT THE AUTHORS

JUDITH L. COLLINGS is the ever-patient companion, helpmeet, and definitively better-half to Michael R. Collings; as such, she was the impetus behind and chief recipe-tester for *Whole Wheat Harvest* (1980), the original incarnation of *Whole Wheat for Food Storage: Recipes for Unground Wheat*.

More importantly, she is the mother of four wonderful children, mother-in-law to four more wonderful children, and grandmother to five (plus one waiting in Heaven). Intensely creative in her own right, she has, over the years, mastered such activities as embroidery, crewel embroidery, counted-cross stitch, stamp-art, and crocheting, and demonstrated her proficiency at beadwork and jewelry design plain and fancy in panels and presentations at a number of fantasy-oriented conferences. Her patience, dedication, and devotion have allowed Professor Collings the time, the leisure, and the luxury to indulge himself in writing. She was the one who instigated the move to their beautiful home in Idaho when Professor Collings retired.

MICHAEL R. COLLINGS is a Professor Emeritus at Seaver College, Pepperdine University, where he directed the Creative Writing Program for over two decades. He has published over 100 volumes of poetry, novels, short fiction, and scholarly studies of such contemporary writers as Stephen King, Orson Scott Card, Dean R. Koontz, and Piers Anthony. Recent works include *The Art and Craft of Poetry (1996, 2009)*; *Toward Other Worlds: Perspectives on John Milton, C. S. Lewis, Stephen King, Orson Scott Card, and Others* (2010); *In Endless Morn of Light: Moral Agency in Milton's Universe* (2010); *In the Void: Poems of Science Fiction, Myth and Fantasy, and Horror (2009)*; *Matrix: Growing Up West—Autobiographical Poems (2010)*; and a Book of Mormon epic, *The Nephiad* (1996, 2010)

His fiction, also published through Wildside, includes: *The House Beyond the Hill: A Novel of Fear (2007)*; *Wordsmith, Volume One: The Thousand Eyes of Flame (2009)* and *Wordsmith, Volume Two: The Veil of Heaven (2009)*; *Singer of Lies: A Science-Fantasy Novel (2009)*; *Wer Means Man, and Other Tales of Wonder and Terror (2010)*; *Three Tales of Omne: A Companion to Wordsmith* (2010); *Devil's Plague: A Mystery Novel (2011)*; and *The Slab (2010),* the story of a haunted tract house in Southern California...that consumes people.

He is now retired and lives in his native state of Idaho.

www.ingramcontent.com/pod-product-compliance
Lightning Source LLC
LaVergne TN
LVHW041630070426
835507LV00008B/535